PENGUIN BOOKS

DRIVERS AT THE SHORT-TIME MOTEL

Eugene Gloria was born in Manila, Philippines, and was raised in San Francisco. He was educated at San Francisco State University, Miami University of Ohio, and the University of Oregon. Gloria received a Fulbright Fellowship in 1992, an artist grant from the San Francisco Art Commission in 1995, 96 Inc.'s Bruce P. Rossley Literary Award, and the Poetry Society of America's George Bogin Memorial Award. He was a scholar at the Bread Loaf Writers' Conference and a resident at the Vermont Studio Center, the Mary Anderson Center for the Arts, and the MacDowell Colony. He lives with his wife, Karen, and teaches at DePauw University in Greencastle, Indiana.

THE NATIONAL POETRY SERIES

The National Poetry Series was established in 1978 to ensure the publication of five poetry books annually through participating publishers. Publication is funded by the late James Michener, the Copernicus Society of America, Edward J. Piszek, the Lannan Foundation, and the National Endowment for the Arts.

1999 COMPETITION WINNERS

Tenaya Darlington of Wisconsin, *Madame Deluxe*
Chosen by Lawson Inada, to be published by Coffee House Press

Eugene Gloria of Massachusetts, *Drivers at the Short-Time Motel*
Chosen by Yusef Komunyakaa, to be published by Penguin Books

Corey Marks of Texas, *Renunciation*
Chosen by Philip Levine, to be published by University of Illinois Press

Dionisio Martinez of Florida, *Climbing Back*
Chosen by Jorie Graham, to be published by W. W. Norton

Standard Schaefer of California, *Nova*
Chosen by Nick Piombino, to be published by Sun & Moon Press

Drivers at the Short-Time Motel

Eugene Gloria

PENGUIN BOOKS

PENGUIN BOOKS
Published by the Penguin Group
Penguin Putnam Inc., 375 Hudson Street,
New York, New York 10014, U.S.A.
Penguin Books Ltd, 27 Wrights Lane,
London W8 5TZ, England
Penguin Books Australia Ltd, Ringwood,
Victoria, Australia
Penguin Books Canada Ltd, 10 Alcorn Avenue,
Toronto, Ontario, Canada M4V 3B2
Penguin Books (N.Z.) Ltd, 182–190 Wairau Road,
Auckland 10, New Zealand

Penguin Books Ltd, Registered Offices:
Harmondsworth, Middlesex, England

First published in Penguin Books 2000

1 3 5 7 9 10 8 6 4 2

Pages 67–68 constitute an extension of this copyright page.

LIBRARY OF CONGRESS CATALOGING-IN-PUBLICATION DATA
Gloria, Eugene.
Drivers at the Short-Time Motel / Eugene Gloria.
p.   cm. — (The national poetry series)
ISBN 0 14 05.8925 2
I. Title.   II. Series.
PS3557.L6485D75   2000
811'.54—dc21
99–054648

Printed in the United States of America
Set in Garamond
Designed by Mia Risberg

for Karen,
my imperial friend,
my most agonizing Spy

No one
to witness
and adjust, no one to drive the car

—William Carlos Williams

Contents

Drivers
at the
Short-Time
Motel

~ Part One ~

In Language

After we make love, I teach you
words I'm slowly forgetting,
names for hands, breast, hair, and river.
And in the telling, I find myself
astonished, recalling the music
in my grandmother's words
before she left this world—
words you don't forget, like a mandate
from heaven. She said, *It's in the act
of cleansing that we kill the spirit—
ourselves; every culture's worst enemy
is its own people.*

And so I teach you, to remind
myself what it means when I say,
hali ka rito, come here, tell me
the names for ocean, stars, river,
and sun—and you tell me
what you remember from the moments
in which the telling arose. You say
hair instead of river; you say breasts
instead of hands; you say
cock and cunt
instead of moon, sea, and stars.

Mauricio's Song

From Mobil Gas he emerges
like a Mack truck from the desert horizon.
You might think of bluefin tunas
coursing the algid sea.
A man with a singular purpose
always walks with his best foot forward—
leans into dusk, moon heavy on his back.
Mauricio has punched out at the station.
If you happen to see him
you might remark on the butterflies—
the small cloud of yellow, speckled wings
fluttering like wayward kites around him.
You might even reconsider
your faith in miracles,
your capacity
to comprehend the mystery.
You could be going to the market
and have already made a list.
You could be as still as a tinsel tree
illuminated by a spinning color wheel
in a room of immobile silhouettes.
You could have your face
pressed against the windowpane—
your chest, a bodiless blouse
and puffy as our Winter faces.
You could be standing in a living room
full of boxes with your fears in tight little bundles.

You could be Mauricio Babilonia
on his way to a rendezvous, his hands
cracked and stained with axle grease,
black as the night gathering at his feet.
And butterflies, impossible and constant,
brushing against his cheeks
like a hundred kisses, the papery wings
of golden monarchs calligraphed
with untranslatable sonnets for one Mauricio Babilonia
on his way to meet his love behind a wall
he will climb, but not fast enough
for the bullet that would seek out his heart.

White Blouses

When *the soul selects her own society,*
she gathers herself like mist
from the rain-drenched earth.
She goes to Texas, orders a steak
with eggs and coffee, drives
a turquoise Cadillac heading for the gulf.
The angels of morphia want to make a home
in the dark cave of the soul's mouth,
they want to crawl
inside a word, which looks more like a road
covered with snow.
Once the soul lay down
on the snow to sleep. She was naked,
weary of making.

Her mouth is pumice white—
not snow, not Hiroshima ash—
but white as a room hoarding all
the neighborhood light,
white as a line of limbless blouses
and bedsheets running through the bluffs
beneath a pale Nebraska sky
where a girl with scoliosis shakes—
working a Hula-Hoop,
like light dancing through a painted window.

Winter Fires

Winter nights in our neighborhood
you can hear the fire engines' wail
clear through the rib cage of every cramped apartment
with at least one space heater set too high.
The village idiots have given up,
tucked in moist blankets.
They've bought this night on credit
beneath great archways of apathetic buildings
with names fat with purchase
like Pillsbury, Madison, and Sutro.
We are recovering from Consumer Credit Counseling.
Our overspent lives read like a broadsheet of debits.

We've been told our future lies in Default, Pennsylvania—
in some trailer park with barking dogs
and corpses of old Chevies.
Could be worse. We could be like our fathers.
Or our great-grandfathers the good children bailed out
time and again from debtors' prison.

The old in our building are prisoners of good manners.
Besides being foolish for not wanting to leave
when the firemen finally came.
They hemmed and hawed, fought with our super.
The weaker ones, those who could no longer fight,
wept beneath their doorways and soaked
their sticky carpets with crocodile tears

when our super ordered all of us
to abandon our homes.

That night the cold swept across our slippered feet,
the fire engines warm and still, their fat hoses
uncoiling from the giant metal spool
as my anthemless neighbors and I stood
clutching our secret possessions pressed
against our breasts as if we were all
pledging allegiance to some cruel god
who stole us away from happy sleep.

Saint Joe
after James Wright

When the choppers churned and swayed
the swift brown current like a field of cogon grasses,
we dropped a rope below,

but the native girl, no older than my daughter,
was too weak to hold on, and let go.
We had to leave her to refuel, though we knew

what the river would do. When my duty was up,
I chose to come here, for humid sheets over bamboo beds,
for some honey in a slip—

a ninety-pound rice cooker named Ronda
and the soap dance she's known to do. But hardly for love,
as I wait with this man bent in my arms.

When the Coca-Cola truck hit this pedicab driver,
you could see his rubber slippers fly
all the way up to the second-floor window.

His body thrown five meters from his cab.
I imagine the Lord Jesus descending from his cross,
a good marine saving the dead in limbo.

But on this god-forgotten street a crowd gathers,
crows peck and gawk, and name me "Joe."
Their faces tell a separate story, each one

ending with the sweet by-and-by, like the girl
whose hands slipped at the end of my rope
dancing above the fury of a bloated river.

A man in a suit slouches off, whistles for a cab;
a flotilla of rubber slippers converges on a two-inch lake of rain.
A pair of white hands, mine, reach for his limp body.

And from the swollen streets, an ambulance calls,
draws closer, louder. And I hold on,
listen to children chant "Joe" in the rain.

Subic Bay

At 12, Lita acts *Imeldific.*
She bats her eyelashes, waxes her lips,
and examines the arc of her mouth
when she says *Oh.*

Her black hair falls over one eye
as she dances on a platform
above a sailor from Norfolk, Virginia,
who will not recognize the hopscotch girl
at the elementary school by the PX.

These night streets are lit by fluorescent
fog lights from platinum jeeps within
a strip, which resembles the flash
of a pinball machine. Street vendors
clang their wares, jarheads in loud
short-sleeved shirts careen toward massage
parlors with two-way mirrors,
women in heavy makeup
wait in well-worn dresses.

In a nightclub, Lita worries
about tomorrow's lesson when
she must conjugate the verb
to be.

Ruin

My beautiful, unlucky brother is a deadbeat,
a scofflaw, a veteran of foreign wars.
When the Vietcong god sent him back to us,
my mother prayed to the Virgin
in repentance for her threat to disown him
when he considered Canada instead of the draft.
In Khe Sanh my brother bivouacked through rice paddies,
though I picture him in rubber slippers
along rice terraces in the Ifugao,
in villages beneath a corrugated sky.
When darkness shut into the dark,
he spied the enemy through his nightscope,
marching like a trail of black ants,
loaded down with light
mortars, scant provisions, and their wounded.

After his tour,
I found a snapshot I wasn't supposed to see—
a captive boy, his ankles held up
by a smiling soldier while another is slicing off his balls.
When my brother had arrived at his manhood,
he called me. It was after the neighborhood boys
gathered before Goteng, a part-time
healer and collector of discarded glass.
Circumcised, my brother, slumped on his bed,
his cock wrapped in guava leaf, and bleeding.

In his hand was a gift, the blue marble,
the one he named the *Conqueror*.

Once there was a bridge
that sagged to the river and beckoned him
to drown with all his gear.
And all the women he had ever loved
would take up his bags and bless his failures,
unpack his last clean shirts—white
like his mestizo skin and delicate as his sisters'.

Beautiful, unlucky brother,
sleepwalking amid the ruins, I call
you back to your desires
along the rim of terraces, back
to the shallow water flourishing with young rice.

"Where the Feeble Senses Fail"
—*Tantum Ergo*

A tight-fisted dowager now in her dotage
inhabits Don Pedro Street like houses
nest in safe little clusters.

She rises before the six o'clock Mass,
before the sparrows twitter their gossip,
before the giant **O** assumes a skin of margarine.

Mother-of-pearl necklace, gold and stoned
brooches of green and ocher, this elderly virgin
made ready for the body of Christ.

Black soot thick as snot smears her hanky
as the Rockwell dust settles atop her
durable wood: objets d'art and antiques from Java.

And like an unexpected phone call,
Bloomington, Indiana, returns as swift as heartbreak
as if heartbreak makes exiles of us all.

And longing for some human hand
allows her to harbor this one secret. In her room
the hi-fi spins a scratched LP with a song

her soldier father would sing,
replete with lament, a ballad to dust
about a doting prodigal finding his way home.

No one will tell him the ship has sailed.
No one to tell him where to lay his hat.
A vendor chants, *Boiled baby duck eggs,*

in her room the record skips, a saved tooth
waits for her father's mortar and pestle,
dark laces clasp her boot with four eyelets,

and tulips in the far Middle West
dress a yard somewhere in Indiana,
some are gold like watches, others pink as blouses.

Song of the Pillar Woman

I. EDSA
We read about a girl in a starched white uniform,
white socks, a Robin-Hood-green ribbon stuck
on her neatly combed hair, on her way to school,
before her picture graced the cover of *Graphic*,

January 5, 1993. She was sprawled on the road—
her life forces flowing, stubborn puddle
of motor grease on the sun-baked macadam,

the Philippine Constabulary, cops in aviator shades
milling about like extras on the set, all so photogenic,
and newsworthy, as this red Pantranco bus
journeys south on Epifanio de los Santos Avenue.

An old woman, barely audible but for the lilt
in her song's saddest part. Her voice falters
and cracks like gears badly meshing

beneath the bus's rusted hood. No one is talking,
not even the *konduktór* folding his small bills
lengthwise: tens round the middle fingers and twenties
make a semi-ring around his pinkies.

A voice, quotidian and homely, whispers:
"*Sayang*, such a shame; a Chinese, only 15.
Her driver, some say, was in cahoots with the PC . . .
There was no other way, they had to kill him, too."

And grandmotherly the singing comes again,
a sparrow's song that modulates and repeats,
singing to us for small change. And ever grateful
for what we can afford to give her,

waves as she alights from the bus in front of Nepa Q Mart.
Pak, pak, the *konduktór* raps the red Pantranco bus
twice on the side to signal our driver to start, and we go
on to our daily offices, on to our private routines.

II. *Lahar*
Moonshock of dunes, ashfalls, mounds of salt,
ancient pillars circled by cicada songs.

I cannot love them, these things I list.
I wait in the church vestibule

amid the vendors and the vagrants you shoo away.
I sell remembrances, medals of the Most Blessed Virgin,

the Sacred Heart, St. Christopher and Child, St. Jude,
and for the afflicted, *the five fingers of the most powerful hand.*

I pin *miraculous medals* on your children's blouses
to save them, God's small artifacts.

On my other job, I wash and iron clothes at your house,
and your girl at the kitchen table listens to her elbow,

waits for a story, which begins:
A woman washed by the sea wears a hairnet of stars . . .

Bathed in yellow from the gas lamp,
I stoop over a narrow board with a wrinkled shirt.

A flatiron commends it new life.
Believe in that mountain burning with dormant love.

Believe in my stories.
Every ending has two versions: each beginning with the sea.

If there were two worlds we are made to inhabit,
I would prefer the one I was forced to leave.

Once rice built a house on 15 hectares of black soil.
Fields steeped in shallow water.

Our devotion to San Isidro yielded 100 cavans of grain.
Pressed against the wall of the house,

a mahogany desk with whorls of faces hardened by varnish,
legs inlaid with squibs of tiny pearls.

Once a woman bent over a man writing at his desk.
A man once held the night in the grip of his pen.

In my story, there are only the medals to wager,
the vagaries of my own conceit,

the small graces I must sell to protect you.
This hand pricked by pins, this ocean of Pinatubo ash.

Once there was a bus bound for the sea.
          Once there was a woman singing of a house.

The Maid

From America my sister writes about the latest action on the wing—
    she lists: lazuli bunting, yellow-breasted chat,
        magpie, tufted titmouse, and vesper sparrow.

Binoculars in one hand, she whiles hours away on winding trails,
    still as a sentinel, serious as a reprimand.
        But here in Manila, where fresh air is as rare as tonic water

and the heat as steady as Kurosawa's rain,
    I've given in to air-conditioned cinemas and crowded malls,
        shoulder to shoulder with the progeny of American TV.

Once a girl in rubber slippers walked into a restaurant
    to order some takeout for her small charge.
        The girl, no more than a child, spied

the room full of oval tables and bright people clad
    in brighter church dresses and Sunday shoes.
        Gaudy matrons with cellular phones

while I, in my polo shirt and penny loafers,
    watched her as my sister would
        trail the still flight of a hummingbird.

If a messenger of the Lord were to intercede and tell this girl
    to walk away and never look back,
        would she vanish into a grain of salt among the nameless?

But when her gaze locked into mine, her eyes widened
    like the mouth of an animal about to swallow its prey—
    they were saying, *I know you, I know you.*

The Driver Conrado's Penitent Life

The scent of food was everywhere he turned,
the vendor stirring his flat black pan,
the scalding oil for the glazed plantains,
and the afternoon darkening like the toll of bells
announcing: time to eat, time to go.
But the driver Conrado was steady
with each pop of the Chiclets he chewed;
a pocket of air would balloon in his mouth
while the boy fidgeted with the radio knob
for some new song his sisters sang.
Conrado, this piece-packing ex-military,
lackey of a petty bureaucrat, Conrado
whose stern eyebrows could answer
yes better than his mouth, Conrado
who would have served time if not for *Sir,*
waits, patient as a sniper.
Beyond the driver was the moon,
and below its fat face stood the school
where inside the bureaucrat was moonlighting
in front of rows of desks, his fingers dusted
with chalk and his mouth drying with words.
What he said to his pupils was difficult
and dull as the distant planets, while the moon
hung brighter than the vendor's lamp.
When the boy's father emerged from the school,
the world turned slightly. Night
became this father of secrets

and all the hard science the boy hungered to master.
The father slumped his wide shoulders forward,
declared to his driver with the authority
that his own class enjoined: *Time to go,*
Conrado, the boy is hungry, it's time we go.

Drivers at the Short-Time Motel

There's a stillness here like in de Chirico's landscapes
of elongated shadows and heat
painted on like egg yolks.
Here, three drivers nap outside the cars they drive,
parked not so much as hull to hull along some make-out point,
but as a fan of two Aces and one Jack,
before the dealer calls them in.
The elder of the three sits on a plastic stool
and sleeps and sleeps.
The other two are matchstick thin
and T-shirted like lumpen prizefighters with towels
tucked in their collars.

In a room inside the tall building,
a woman in white chemise nods on the arm of a man
in a suit too tight in the elbows.
He could be my father
and she his mistress, an accountant,
a termagant or typist,
or a stylist at Zenny's House of Beauty.

Let the chauffeurs sleep
through rain and sun, rain and sun
in this country of fits and starts. Let them sleep
outside of history,
outside of this cacique democracy.
They are not capos of warlords,

not gatekeepers of gilded subdivisions.
The drivers are like the bride
in the story who sleeps on the pillow of her arms
in a diner somewhere in Alabama,
while her groom drives away in a car
rattling like tin cans in the rain.

The House in San Miguel

I'd rather tell you that I am weeping
over a poem by Chong Lau about a man
without a country, mourning his wife,
than admit that I am waiting
for a warm hand against my cheek
like the touch of a lovesick
spirit who startled a maid
in the keep of sleeping strangers.
I am waiting for this woman whose ghost
wanders through this house, how she,
according to legend, was seen standing
before an old bureau where she hid
precious coins for those she'd chosen,
open channels in the chink of eternity.
But night is long and no one comes.
Only sleep as I slump into a dream
about a man saying good-bye to his father
whose face is neither mine nor my father's,
like the flowers I've gathered but cannot name.
I recall every wayward mark, each lesion
on his face, the unbearable radiance
surrounding him when he speaks of trials,
which draw him closer to his god.
When I awake, I think of my mother's
brother in his august years. I remember
the surgery to his eyes, which gave back
his sight, an inverse of Paul whose lack of faith

was wakened by blindness.
My uncle has made some mistakes—
poor manager of a luckless life.
He and others like him have lost
by design of an ill-starred birth
but learned the most by failing.
In the poorly lit avenues
we inhabit in dreams, my dead uncle
wanders quietly, searching for his clothes.
But nothing close to restless spirits
shawled in luminescence comes to me,
neither scent of candles, *damas de noche,*
nor what would serve as a sign
for my own passing: peeled tangerines
scenting the open window.
This morning I wake with clarity
sharp as the pitch of five hundred roosters
laying claim to this godless hour.
I will arise and go now,
find my way to my father's house.

~ Part Two ~

For the Dead and What's Inside Us

My father, in all his singularity,
stands before the bluegreen lawn
in the middle of a drought.
I watch the night my father has become—
I am his shadow, a watcher of night.
From far away, their telephone rings,
my mother tells me Tio Claro died in sleep.
When he was buried, helicopters dropped
petals of *ilang-ilang;* they fell like beads
of fragrant rain. In my dream,
naked soldiers waist-deep in water
shoot at the sky, and clouds
give way to a monsoon of flowers.
A boy who knows nothing
asks his father questions,
his sentences shaped from a wilderness of interrogatives.
How many stars are there in the night?
To whom does God pray? Does He ever sleep?
Why did Judas hang himself?
My father, who never disappoints, replies
with a story about night stars and betrayal,
how Judas smiled at heaven before hanging himself,
and how the pieces of silver, which fell from his purse,
became a new constellation. In the valley of dry hills,
a developer's dream of identical houses,
my father recalls the banks of the Pasig
launching a fleet of paper ships.

Tio Claro returns from America
with his book retelling his life as a soldier.
My father, the younger brother who stayed behind,
imagines himself among faraway stars,
crafts stories that will give way to explanations and subterfuge.
But tonight, there is this lawn
in Northern California, there is this man
who must tend to it, make it live
so he will not think about his own passing.
When I speak with him, my father sounds distant,
his throat parched from not speaking.
I ask him questions, he clears his voice,
says nothing, his silence
the very shape of our distance.

On Mission Road

Near Home Sausage Factory
we stand outside the yellow cab.
My sisters, brothers, and all our lives'
belongings piled on the curb. Only yesterday
we had gathered for a photograph
at the Manila Airport with my grandmother
and the priest my sister had a crush on.
I recall my grandmother's warm breath
as she whispered something slowly,
each word calming the turbulent waves
in my dreams where my family,
in a long narrow boat, sails for America.
I dreamed over and over my death
from drowning, eight eternal seconds,
swallowing water on a beach in Lingayen.

I am here now, my feet planted on Mission Street,
my father insisting Mission *Road*
to the cabby whose hand, gnarled in a fist,
glided toward me and blossomed open
to receive crisp dollar bills.
The cabby had driven us to our destination,
unloaded our luggage, understood his role
as did Conrado who drove my father for a living
in our '62 Bel Air, Conrado
who owed him loyalty, *utang na loob,*
a debt of gratitude for his first real job.

The cabby left us simply this,
service rendered, though I saw him half-turn
and look at us once more before driving off.

Iron Man

What would the dingy white walls be
without the girls in string bikinis circa 1973?

A late afternoon light sliced in two,
maybe three, triangles and a length of shadow,
a dark peninsula in this oily lube bay
smelling of old tires and motor grease.

Gargoyle-heavy and gray as highways he yawns:
My great idiot the moon is a giant onion my heart
gnaws and gnaws. Beating his breast
in mea culpa fashion, he then belches.

My lord of facts luxuriates
in mundane purchases at Napa Auto Parts.
Today he's bagged a muffler, two gaskets,
hex nuts and stove bolts specific to the make and year.

He is the Lally pole that ballasts
the woodbeams of our happy home.
Married twice for love
(my mom his first), he cheated and never lost.

My great provider is as loveless as a kitchen stool.
Yet, he maps out my life like an architect
who can read the blueprints to the pleasure palace
floating in the air. At his garage a customer waits,

an old distinguished man with a portmanteau name
(something like Giancarlo or Juan Maria),
with a portable chair that folds up into a working cane.
Beneath the hoary light he sits,

watches my father fit the roughened gloves
big as oven mittens over his fat, white knuckles,
clutch the stems of welding rods, and drop
the welder's helmet over his face with a nod.

A hiss of gas and his Zippo lighter clicks,
and then a snap of white to blue to yellow burns
as he mends the hairline fracture of the car's
noisy exhaust nearly rusted to the core.

Like an old villain in a comic book,
my father is iron-masked and gowned in sparks.

Milkfish

You feed us milkfish stew
and long grain rice, make us eat
blood soup with chili peppers,
and frown at us when we lose our appetite.
I remember when I was young and you told me
of that monsoon: the Japanese Occupation—
stories of a time before you met my father,
when you learned the language of an occupied city
in order to feed your family.
You were the pretty one at seventeen,
your skin, white as milkfish.
The pretty ones, you said,
were always given more food—
the Japanese soldiers sentried
above the loft where you worked
dropped sweet yams, and you caught them
by the billow of your skirt.
I remember you in sepia-brown photographs
as a mestiza who equated liberation
with Hershey bars and beige nylons from American GIs—
and the season of the monsoon as dark as hunger
was not about suffering
but what you knew of beauty.

The Whisper

In the ripest days of August,
sunflowers droop their heavy heads as if listening.
It was from such a posture
that my Lolo Panta learned those words
he mumbled over fetishes,
over tonics he concocted,
over the ache of muscles and high fevers,
over neatly folded clothes he kept
in dresser drawers rank
with the smell of church candles and wood.
At his last hour, Lolo Panta lay
longing for his children, a white
handkerchief folded in a band around his throat
like Father Tiodoro's collar,
concealing the hole round as Communion hosts.
When his house on Avenida Rizal
was empty except for his dog,
Lolo Panta would sneak a Salem menthol
and drag a rich lungful through the hole,
exhaling his forbidden pleasure
with eyes clenched shut.
                              Years after my lolo died,
my mother told me with indifference
about *dwendes:* the black and the white
born from the belly of the soil.
Their mischief akin to *mangkukulams,*
those who hold life in the blink of an eye,

or a curse—like the Virgin of Guadalupe,
trampling the heads of snakes.
My lolo healed victims of spells by blessing
his amulets: small pieces of wood
carved with the sign of the cross.
He would burn them, then wait for the spirit's face
to appear in the screen of white smoke.
He'd melt candles for expectant mothers
and with the wax determine the sex of the child.
                        My mother was my lolo's
third child, born between a sister who died at birth
and a brother who died in his second summer.
She inherited by virtue of surviving
the power to heal with touch,
the smooth glide of hands against skin and sore limbs,
the hard grind of her open palms,
fingers working in saliva,
or the aroma of Vicks VapoRub.
                        When the mounds of earth
where *dwendes* lived were leveled and replaced
by buildings and new houses, my mother found
a job at Travelers Life answering phones.
The language of the village withered inside her
when she took up the voice of American movies.
And the spirits of the siblings she was born between
hid away beneath the river.
                        In his final hour,
inside the room where he once parceled
powdered cures in small brown envelopes,
Lolo Panta bent in the sunburnt heat
and whispered the words to his dog beside him.

Later the dog trotted away sniffing at the mounds
behind my lolo's house, and my mother
began her long workday as usual.

Nocturne: Two Versions

1. Draft
My brother and I stare at the seasick boats
and the picnickers on the grass.
He lights a cigarette. Last thing of his
besides a busted marriage.

Topaz sun and fuchsia sky
conspire in a brilliant but fading light.
The color of my mother's chiffon dress,

layers of softness like a John F. Kennedy rose.
We will not speak of wars inside of us
when America unfolded like my grade-school primer.

The war, mythic at first when I was ten,
became our war: my brother fighting an enemy
who looked more like us than the soldiers
he bunked with in boot camp.

After twenty years, my brother is not free
to speak of those things we gloss over
amid the hum and flicker of our parents'
television during Thanksgiving dinner.

Smoke from our cigarettes fills us like stories.
This afternoon we watch a family, newcomers,
eating steamed rice and Kentucky Fried Chicken.

Posing for a photograph, their shameless joy,
the crispness of their knockoff Guess jeans,
and their ungainly aunt who petitioned them here.

My brother grunts, *Flips. Fuck, I hate them.*
I recall a photograph, the two of us beside this same bay,
its color fading like the last good light of day.

2. Revision
From the pedicab a sea of blue
uniformed men hold fort outside a bank.
My brother is not among them.

But I think of him as I watch these gaunt,
angular guards dawdle in their starched blues.
My eyes drink the blue of their uniform,

serious as money, serious as my brother's dress blues
he wore when he came home after the war,
after grandmother lived with us, after Nixon quit.

We heard Mass, and mother knelt before a list of names
in a dark corner of the church. My brother Jose
dignified in bold type: private first class,

GI Joe Marine. Once a guard at Binh Thuy Bridge,
my brother spoke the idiom of Mississippi
blacks, the grammar of military English.

Joe sucked the metal of his .45 when his wife left,
put the gun down, then found the tune of *Mistah Charlie*
in the somber iambs of jarheads called upon by America.

Semper Fi, little bro'. *Semper Fi*, mothafuckas.
In Manila, I picture my brother
on his pedicab hustling for fares, while this sky

ignited like the fire tonguing the tip of his cigarette.
And in the slow exhale of day cooling into night,
darkness fell upon him like light.

Sisters of the Poor Clares

Wednesdays before the noon hour, nuns in bloomers
play volleyball beside our schoolyard.

Our lessons punctuated by the thud of a knife-hand serve,
hurtling ball over net, trailed by wicked shrills,

the contact of hand and ball as we shut our books for recess.
I've often wondered how they dressed

in their daily offices, pressing unleavened bread
for Communion hosts. In the chapel,

Monsignor Kenney says Mass twice a week
for the tin full of wafers he'll take back to his parish.

Once, through screened partitions I heard them sing—
their voices rising like incense smoke

spiraling toward heaven. From the vestibule
I watched their alabaster forms, bunched

in a row of shorter pews, gilded flowers, white lilies—
the Poor Clares, their task of praying for the world.

Pan de Sal

He is among the sleepless angels revising his life,
his bony cheeks drummed in and drummed out.
Like a lesser monk he clasps his hands,

shuts his eyes, light dimming inside him.
He recalls the morning scent of *pan de sal*
cradled in his arms along the pebbly road.

The smell of bread as strong as hunger
stirs him away from his vanishing.
The bread had broken through the paper sack,

and he remembers bending over to pick them up
as they gathered dirt. Soil and salt, desire and descent.
Did the earth love the *pan de sal*

enough to summon them from his arms?
Through a line of many colored shirts
and bright underpants of the immigrant neighbor,

he will consider the stars, believe
that they will love him enough like gravity.
Desire and descent, this prodigal night.

Maybe his great fall is in remembering that first kiss
when he was seven and the other boy, only five—
maybe in that first kiss he is forgiven,
because he wants forgiveness, wants always to be loved.

Elegy for No One

When the cancer took hold of Conrado's bad eye,
it flowered into a lump of raw flesh.
His old friends paid him a visit, then convened
with their expert diagnoses:
probably a hot starter. We'll let his engine cool,
then crank him up again.
No, the other chimed, his plugs are shot,
his points and condensers need tuning.
But the elder mechanic, a clairvoyant of sorts,
spelled out his opinion this way:
My friends, it is the water.
Water has rusted through the core of his soul.
A short pause followed, then each one,
in his distinct gesture, reached for a stick
of Kool or Camel and lit the fag end
with his Zippo or Bic.
I see . . . the water, the youngest of the three
said softly with a cloud
streaming from his ovaled lips
as if lost in some culvert of memory.

A black Ford station wagon ferried
the driver Conrado's remains
like a barge on a river of jeepneys.
There was no vigil, no ceremony, no service,
no band of senior citizens droning a dirge.
No paper money scattered on the street.

No incense, no wax dripping
on pants and shoelaces.
No soldiers with shiny brass buttons,
no cops in aviator shades,
no slick strangers in long coats with epaulets,
no ex-nuns and ex-priests and ex-revolutionaries.
No Rubenesque soprano singing a Schubert song.
No ministers of finance, no fathers with fat asses,
no matrons with Coach handbags and cellular phones.
No college co-eds with bandeaux and scrunchies.
No hipster professors with arcane degrees.
No news on CNN, no report on the local TV.
No one to witness
and adjust, no one to drive the car.

~ Part Three ~

Palawan

In Sabang an outrigger ferried us
to the leeward side of the island.
A boatman waited to carry us inside

the cave where you hear only the asthmatic
breathing of the gas lamp and the oar's
steady clap against the underground water.

Interior river leading to an interior sea,
Palawan, island of lepers and refugees,
island of dogs and bird-nest poachers.

Palawan, an island in the South China Sea,
where a man with a knife wound lay
in a state of mute grace—his body half-

abandoned, half-redeemed by a woman
combing sweat from his hair
in our jeepney clouded with dust.

Her man's story begins and ends with blood.
His knife, his pride, this idiot thing
he flails like a drunk fumbling for his keys—

a fish vendor posing like a street-corner thug.
Not touching, we lay on our narrow bed.
It was the first night of my wife's menstrual flow,

blood passing through her in slow rivulets.
The simple terrors we invent, the names we give
for our fears: Dalkiel, prince of dogs,

Aziel, lord of knives, this room, our darkest night.
I will betray my wife, and one day she will leave.
When the moon waxes yellow, there is no balm

strong enough to soothe a lover's wound.
The howling of dogs suddenly stopped,
our room now silent, except for the oar

beneath that cave we dreamed of for weeks
with cathedral-tall rocks like deformed wax statues.
In a few hours it would be sunrise.

But we would've already awakened, our packs
and satchels ready. The only jeepney out
would leave at five for Puerto Princesa.

Over unpaved roads we soldier the long ride,
our driver is a terrible angel who hums a bad tune.
A woman sleeps, her face pressed against the smell of rust.

Rizal's Ghost

Once on a train from Baden-Baden,
fields beneath gray skies

looked like loneliness that made you strong.
A staccato of steel against grinding steel,

each lurch, each shove of that swift machine
became one thought and then another,

an intaglio of memory pressed
against a sheet of layered landscapes:

that first sunrise burning through a net
of tule fog in the Sacramento Delta;

that once I slept on damp night grass
and drowned beneath an ocean of stars.

I'd cut my hand in Baden-Baden,
sucked blood from the same hand

in Nice: the bread, the brie,
the cold slice of salami

salted from my blood-stained knife.
I recalled the flowers from Heidelberg,

fragrantless and flat between
Jose Rizal's journal: the petal's cup,

violet and white, so kind to his eyes.
Once in the Black Forest I unfolded

my handkerchief in which I had taken
dark bread from my hostel's table.

As I moistened it with rain,
Jose Rizal's ghost crossed

my wooded path, a purple flower
in one hand, a clean bullet hole

through his breast. A broken whisper
breathed from his ashen lips. *Never forget*

this flower, he began in sotto voce,
Never forget the sky which saw its birth.

I grasped the flower from his hand,
the moistened bread I left in his.

I passed two hikers on my way,
their voices thick as the knapsacks

they carried. They were Americans,
their language for a moment unlike my own.

News of Pol Pot's Capture

That night the moon over New Hampshire
wore a face I knew in high school
of a pudgy boy whose mother was a singer
and whose sister was once trapped
in a burning building. When she was a girl,
my sister and 17 of her classmates
could not leave school
because the janitor ran amok.

The moonlight on the lake glides
like Persian slippers wingtipping
on the surface of the water.
And the road with its arms
around the lake is silent and American.
In Thai, *Sasithon* stands for full moon,
a name for a woman who once saw a pair of hands
on the dashboard of my car.
Not hers, but of another who died a violent death.

In the whir of static
between Top Forty and twang, I listened
to the news report of Pol Pot's capture.
And like a man whose bowl of soup
has grown too cold to eat,
I realized that I had overdriven—
missed the road I was supposed to turn into.
In a false memory, I look back

at the burning building
that claimed my classmate's sister.
I see her moonface veiled in blue—
blue as the flame of a lit match
telling me the road I missed on the map.
I could pull over and rest my eyes.

I could sleep like an entire race
of bones underneath the tall grasses
where a man hacks and hacks
at something in the heat.
Once in a while he might stop
to examine the pattern of a tattered fabric
suspended on the tip of his machete,
and try to remember his wife.

Sweet Talk

The stone buttoned on your ear
is green as beans, and bright as fireflies.
It is Friday, May, dinner is on me.

You had snagged a job in a factory,
inspecting commas and clauses
with overschooled spouses of preachers and clerks.

And the night sky I commit to memory
smells like sachets of purple violets
pinned on camisole straps of apologetic aunts.

Tonight, May blossoms droop like copper Slinkies
on hedges fencing the parish rectory
where the dopey prelate takes his tea and cake.

When we met, I confessed my mental block with tenses—
something you, dear, mistook for ethnic time.
And as things happen,

confessions turn into sweet talk,
in the same way you recall your mother clipping lilacs
and stuffing them in clumsy jam jars

atop your father's console playing Schumann or Bach.
Lilacs on dressers, on nightstands, adorning toilet tanks.
I know all this by heart like stories we breathe.

Friday, May, an occasion for joy,
random as grace; and on your ear,
the emerald's green light, a near-distant star.

Palm Sunday

Always the sky keeps expanding.
Wide as America's brave margins,
wide as my loneliness in the Middle West.
I lean against a dust cloud behind us,
the glory sinking into a muted timberline.
I am drunk with longing. The wind is singing—

my drunken friend, the wind, hurls
sweet curses at my face.
We have learned to love
this road, which lies down like pythons,
refuses to forgive our excesses,
refuses to consider us kin. Our driver's

sign overhead reads, *Jesus is my co-pilot.*
Jesus who crossed the city
gates of his ancestors
on a road carpeted by palms.
Our goodtime driver must know this—
he drives with abandon,

despite our fragile cargo: scholars and accountants,
prophets and exiles all the same to him.
The road, which suggests things, is tired of ceremony.
It lies down to sleep like the snow.
Lie down TallMountain, lie down
Serafin Syquia, lie down Li-Young, lie

down Divakaruni, lie down Eman Lacaba,
lie down pilgrims of the open road.
Shameless, we gather our light
jackets in balls. We rest our heads,
our faces upturned to a squall of stars.
I near the end, my soul recites.

O loneliness, my body responds.
This empty road is a house
where no one lives. What strange fire
we bring when we come to this house.

Carlos Bulosan

I am through with you, Carlos Bulosan—
tired of listening for the footfalls
of light leading toward this switchback of words
you string like a necklace of *ling ling o.*

I am through with you, Carlos Bulosan,
clambering at the door only to find the ghost
of your lost manuscript scattered on my floor.
I didn't make it to Mangusmana,
but found my name along the Dinalaoan

where a dirt road elbows into another
and a row of nipa huts active with kilns
burning wood beneath houses on stilts,
smoke seeping through wide slats
of bamboo where my cousins spread

their sleep mats and drape clouds
of mosquito nets at night.
Clear through the haze below,
where pigs and chickens reign,

my aunts and their daughters
busy themselves with banana leaves,
separating them sheet by leafy sheet
for the tiny white moons

sweet and abundant as love
my small nieces showered when I came
to visit and brag of my country
that denies me
and has denied you, Carlos Bulosan,

brother of the dirt
and the Imperial Valley Asparagus.
Lover of fat hips and all
that is sensual in the white women
you loved when they held your face

in the dull light of a Delano bunkhouse,
or was it in Turlock or Tacoma, far
from the country of a thousand smiles
and the strongly devoted,
far from the palmsap wine the rebels drank—.

Tonight I recall the song
of the old woman combing the thick
hanks of her daughter's hair, remember
only the part about the greeny water

where the village madwoman,
fatigued and lovelorn, bathed one night
in the cool Dinalaoan.
She died, the old woman sang,
because the river took pity on her.

Here is my hand, Carlos Bulosan,
I make this pact with you.

Let no anthem well within us,
let the moon which owns nothing have our names.

Let this common face
we wear, dark and inconsolable,
be our only cargo.

White Flower

In a cul-de-sac valley,
a woman's hand smooths petals,
then clips thorned stems
she'll arrange in a choir of roses.

Out back is her husband lost
in the long ago as he scoops
a fistful of earth to plant seedlings
of peach, or plum, he no longer remembers.

But the husband recalls
what he refuses to forget of the hot months
before the vagrant rains in July,

before the small flat
where nights his children slept
side by side on straw mats spread on the floor,

and in a separate room,
desire's cries muffled to a hush.

What the husband remembers
is his boyhood town
and the history of his heart

where once a woman in a light
summer dress and borrowed high heels

came to visit and never returned
to the city where she's from.

This is the story he unearths
from the wilderness within.
A story about winning
this woman's hand
after showing her the old church
and the choir loft where he sang.

Legend has it that elopement
is another's word for abduction,
this woman's version, perhaps not as sweet.

I recall my father's story
and retell it to my lover
as we walk through paved streets
I can no longer name.

Tonight my sleeping lover's body
shapes the sheet covering her.
She is tossing and churning in a storm
of uneasy sleep. I pause from writing,

wake her with my boathand
sailing over waves of shadowed sinews,
the ripples of her spine,
muscle and skin against skin.

My fingertips oiled with White Flower:
pungent cure-all for the body's pain,
except for the boneache of sweet desire.

Once there was a man who palmed seeds
on smooth earth as if they were memories,
and a woman's tenderest hands gave in to love.

The Buick

Inside the full center of afternoon, a man
sets off toward the bridge arcing over gray water.
He grips the wheel, white knuckles exposed.
Two figures drawn in light, a man and his shadow
locked in their careless moorings.
Years ago, he saw a woman hanging on to life
quickly expiring like words taken by the wind.
She was in her Buick lying on its side
like a beached seal, or a fat rabbit
lounging L-shaped after its meal of hay.
The woman's lower lip nearly sliced off
was suspended by a thin thread of saliva.
She was trying to say something
from her impossible position.
                              Down East,
in Ellsworth or Hancock, where she lived as a girl,
stands a line of apple trees,
Empire, Granny Smith, Northern Spy,
blossoming with white flowers.
And the man remembers a boy standing
beside a car door swung open, his lips moving,
in what later he would describe as prayer—
to be anywhere but here.

Within this empty hour, a man wades
through a flood of memory, migrant and various.
A sister's dress translucent in the harsh afternoon light,

the neon fields of Scotch broom in Half Moon Bay,
a wall of tule fog like blindness on the solitary highway.
Empire night, father of vague inheritances,
mayor of lost souls, overlord of the invisible.
                              He eases his grip on the wheel,
because the orange light has gathered in his hands.
And to no one, he mutters: I remain
in the stink of my skin, I lie on the back of a hyphen.
And what is constant and what returns
like the thud of an old screen door is the woman's voice,
the wheels of her Buick spinning in the air;
she was trying to tell him something,
say something incomprehensible and sad.

Acknowledgments

Grateful acknowledgment is made to the editors and publishers of the following periodicals and anthologies in which some of the poems in this collection were first published, sometimes in different versions:

96 Inc.: "Iron Man"
Asian Pacific American Journal: "Palawan" (formerly "Blood"), "White Flower," and "The House in San Miguel"
Blue Mesa Review: "Milkfish"
Crab Orchard Review: "News of Pol Pot's Capture"
Greensboro Review: "For the Dead and What's Inside Us"
Gulf Coast: "Mauricio's Song" and "Winter Fires"
Madison Review: "The Buick"
Mid-American Review: "Rizal's Ghost"
Parnassus: Poetry in Review: "Subic Bay"
Willow Springs: "White Blouses"

"The Whisper," "In Language," and "Milkfish" appeared in *The Open Boat: Poems from Asian America*, edited by Garrett Hongo (New York: Anchor/Doubleday, 1993).
"On Mission Road" appeared in *Dissident Song: A Contemporary Asian American Anthology*, edited by Marilyn Chin (Santa Cruz, Calif.: *Quarry West*, 1992).
"Rizal's Ghost" appeared in *Returning a Borrowed Tongue*, edited by Nick Carbó (Minneapolis: Coffee House Press, 1996).

"Sisters of the Poor Clares" appeared in *The Anthology of New England Writers*, edited by Frank Anthony (Windsor, Vt.: New England Writers Association, 1996).

"Carlos Bulosan" and "Palm Sunday" appeared in *Flippin': Filipinos Writing on America*, edited by Luis Francia and Eric Gamalinda (New Brunswick, N.J.: Rutgers University Press, 1997).

"The Driver Conrado's Penitent Life" and "The Maid" will appear in *Tilting the Continent: Southeast Asian American Literature*, edited by Shirley Geok-lin Lim (Minneapolis: New Rivers Press, 2000).

Thanks also to the San Francisco Art Commission for the timely encouragement represented by the grant and to the Mary Anderson Center for the Arts, the Vermont Studio Center, and the MacDowell Colony for the luxury of space and silence, which allowed me to work on these poems.

I am deeply grateful to those who have helped me shape the poems in this collection: Garrett Hongo, Robert Wrigley, Corrinne Hales, Eric Gamalinda, Eve Wood, Sandy Brown, Kristen Lindquist, Janet Kaplan, Carol Potter, and Karen Singson.

Finally, I wish to express my gratitude to Paul Slovak at Penguin, to Robert Wrigley who helped keep hope alive, to Garrett Hongo for his guidance and tenderness, and especially to Yusef Komunyakaa for taking notice.